⊕ WORLD BOOK'S
CELEBRATIONS AND RITUALS AROUND THE WORLD

World Book, Inc.

a Scott Fetzer Company

Chicago

This edition published in the United States of America by World Book, Inc., Chicago.
WORLD BOOK and the GLOBE DEVICE are registered trademarks or trademarks of World Book, Inc.

World Book, Inc.
233 North Michigan Avenue
Chicago, IL 60601 U.S.A.

For information about other World Book publications, visit our Web site http://www.worldbook.com, or call 1-800-WORLDBK (967-5325).
For information about sales to schools and libraries, call:
1-800-975-3250 (United States); 1-800-837-5365 (Canada).

In the same series:
New Year's Celebrations
Harvest Celebrations
National Celebrations
Spring Celebrations

Copyright © 2003, McRae Books Srl

Via dei Rustici, 5—Florence, Italy.
info@mcraebooks.com

Library of Congress Cataloging-in-Publication Data
Birth and growing up celebrations.
    p. cm.—(World Book's celebrations and rituals around the world)
  Summary: Relates the history of childhood and describes how birth, coming of age, and other important childhood events are celebrated in different countries and by different cultures around the world. Includes recipes and activities.
  ISBN 0-7166-5010-X
  1. Birth customs—Cross-cultural studies—Juvenile literature. 2. Children—Religious life—Cross-cultural studies—Juvenile literature. 3. Rites and ceremonies—Cross-cultural studies—Juvenile literature. [1. Birth customs. 2. Coming of age. 3. Rites and ceremonies.] I. World Book, Inc. II. Series.
GT2460 .B58 2002
392.1'2—dc21   2002027031

Printed and bound in Hong Kong by C&C Offset
1 2 3 4 5 6 7 8 9 10 09 08 07 06 05 04 03 02

McRae Books:
Publishers: Anne McRae and Marco Nardi
Series Editor: Loredana Agosta
Graphic Design: Marco Nardi
Layout: Sebastiano Ranchetti
Picture Research: Laura Ottina, Loredana Agosta
Cutouts: Filippo delle Monache, Alman Graphic Design
Text: Matilde Bardi p. 7; Catherine Chambers pp. 36–41; Anita Ganeri pp. 10–23; Hazel Mary Martell pp. 30–35, 42–43; Claire Moore pp. 8–11

Illustrations: Inklink Firenze, Studio Stalio (Alessandro Cantucci, Fabiano Fabbrucci, Andrea Morandi, Ivan Stalio), Paola Ravaglia, Paula Holguin, Antonella Pastorelli

Color Separations: Litocolor, Florence (Italy)

World Book:
Editorial: Maureen Liebenson, Sharon Nowakowski
Research: Paul Kobasa, Cheryl Graham
Text Processing: Curley Hunter, Gwendolyn Johnson
Proofreading: Anne Dillon

Acknowledgements
The Publishers would like to thank the following photographers and picture libraries for the photos used in this book.
t=top; tl=top left; tc=top center; tr=top right; c=center; cl=center left; cr=center right; b= bottom; bl=bottom left; bc=bottom center; br=bottom right
A.S.A.P Picture Library: 25c; Corbis/De Bellis: 15cl, 15bl; Corbis/Grazia Neri: 17tr, 18cl, 18br, 19tc, 19cr, 43tl; Dinodia: 21b; Lonely Planet Images: Sara Jane Cleland 23bl, Alex Dissanayake 37t, Adrien Vadrot 37b; Marco Lanza: 11br, 13cl, 29cl, 24tr; The Image Works: 6cr, 14c, 22b, 23cr, 26tr, 27bl, 28b, 29tr, 30c, 31tr, 31b, 32tr, 32b, 33c, 34br, 38tr, 38b, 39br, 40c, 41tr, 41cl

⬤ W O R L D   B O O K ' S
CELEBRATIONS AND RITUALS AROUND THE WORLD

BIRTH AND GROWING UP
CELEBRATIONS

Table of Contents

Ancient Celebrations

The Far East

South and Central Asia

The Middle East

Europe and the Americas

Africa

Australasia and Oceania

Glossary

Index

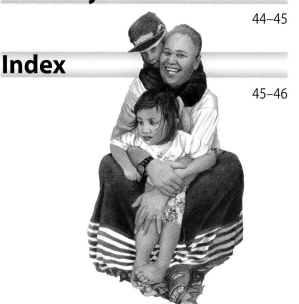

Introduction

The arrival of a new baby causes joy and festivities in nearly every human society. The period leading up to birth is also a special time for many people, with prayers or protective rites and ceremonies carried out for the mother-to-be and her child. In many traditional societies, the birth itself is accompanied by such rituals and precautions as chanting or reciting from sacred texts or smearing the newborn baby with animal fat to protect it from evil spirits. In many cases, the new mother and her child live separately from the main community for a short time after the birth. This period is usually referred to as a time of purification, although it may be a sensible way to shield the baby from contact with potentially harmful germs until it gains strength and resistance.

In nearly all societies, ceremonies called rites of passage mark a child's growth to adulthood. A naming ceremony usually ranks first among these rites. At this ceremony, a child not only receives a name, but also becomes a formal member of the society into which he or she was born. Infant baptism is one example of a naming ceremony. Another major rite of passage usually involves becoming or being recognized as an adult within the group. Every culture has its own special adult initiation rites. These range from graduating from high school or college in the United States, to surviving alone in the wild for several weeks in Papua New Guinea.

This handcarved, ivory Ikhoko pendant was worn by Pende boys of central Africa during their initiation ceremonies to protect them from evil spirits.

Deerskin dolls made by American Indian Sioux women were a favorite plaything for young girls. They also prepared for their future roles by playing with toy tepees.

A Japanese inubako dog doll symbolized children growing up in good health. It often was placed at the bedside of women giving birth and next to the cradles of newborn babies. The dog also was thought to ward off evil spirits.

GROWING UP AROUND THE WORLD

Age 1
The Chinese Zhuazhou ceremony celebrates a child's first birthday.

Age 3
A child celebrates his or her first Shichi-go-san (7-5-3) festival in Japan. Jewish boys first wear a skullcap called a yarmulka or a kippah.

Age 5
The Hindu Vidyarambha samskara is performed.

Age 8
African girls may begin domestic training.

Age 10
Aboriginal boys begin the initiation ritual.

Age 11
Boys attend a Shinbyu ceremony in Myanmar.

Age 12
Sikh children attend a turban-tying ceremony. A Jewish girl has her bat mitzvah at age 12 or 13.

Age 13
A Jewish boy has his bar mitzvah.

Age 15
An Hispanic girl has a Quiceañera ceremony.

Age 18
Many young adults around the world can begin voting.

Age 20
A Seijin-no-hi coming-of-age ceremony is held in Japan.

Taweret (also called Thoueris), the goddess and protector of pregnant women in ancient Egypt, appeared as a combination of hippopotamus, lion, and crocodile.

The ancient Egyptian goddess Isis, protector of women in childbirth, holds her son Horus.

Ancient Celebrations

A maid servant passes a baby to its mother in this ancient Greek engraving.

Childhood Ceremonies in the Ancient World

In ancient times, childbirth was much more dangerous than it is today. Many mothers and children died. So the healthy birth of a child was cause for celebration, usually involving religious rituals. In many cultures, people believed that blessing and purifying newborn children would help them on their journey through childhood.

This woman is shown giving birth in an Egyptian birth box, right, with the help of Hathor, the cow-headed goddess of fertility, on each side.

Ancient Egypt

The ancient Egyptians worshiped gods of fertility, such as Hathor, Isis, Bes, and Taweret, who were believed to protect women in childbirth. Statues of these deities were present at a birth to protect mother and child from harm. Egyptian women gave birth in special birth boxes. When the baby was born, both mother and child would remain in seclusion for two weeks. During this time, the new mother underwent a purification ritual before being allowed to rejoin the community. Babies in ancient Egypt often died, and so spells and dances were performed to safeguard them.

Artemis, right, *the goddess of childbirth, was worshiped by Greek women.*

Ancient Greece

Most Greek women gave birth at home with the help of female friends and neighbors or a midwife. An olive wreath hanging on the door of the house announced the birth of a boy. A hunk of wool told the community the baby was a girl. After giving birth, women often visited the shrines of the goddesses of childbirth, Artemis and Ilithyia, to give thanks for a safe delivery.

Coming of Age in Greece

Several rituals marked the transition from childhood to adulthood in ancient Greece. Agoge (formal upbringing) began around age 7. For boys, it involved having a haircut, and it meant preparing for military training. The arkteia (bear ritual) announced that a girl was ready for marriage and motherhood. Girls participated in special dances and ran races to honor Artemis, the goddess of purity and childbirth.

A berserk warrior wrestles with a bear, one of the tests of courage and physical strength required to enter this warrior band. Berserkers were devoted to Odin, the Norse god of war.

Becoming a Norse Warrior

The Norse Vikings used runes (letters of the Germanic alphabet) at birth to find a name and predict the destiny of a newborn child. Seven days later, a simple and joyful ceremony granted the child nonadult membership in a clan. This status lasted until the child became an adult during a formal initiation ceremony. For a young man, initiation into the feared band of warriors called the berserkers was an important coming-of-age rite.

Newborns of Ancient Rome

In ancient Rome, the father traditionally raised a newborn baby in the air as a sign of his acceptance of the child. Girls received a name eight days after their birth, while boys got theirs a day later.

The Celts

Ancient Celtic rituals were closely linked to nature, and birth was celebrated as the renewal of life. Births were often attended by a Druid or clan healer, who anointed the baby with sacred oils to bless and purify the child. The new mother often ate salmon, apple, and hazelnuts, and then received a blessing. Celtic mother goddesses were widely worshiped, appearing as a trio.

In a trio of Celtic mother goddesses, each goddess holds a symbol of fertility, such as a cloth, napkin, sponge, basket of fruit and bread, or a baby.

Chalchiuhtlicue

Among the Aztecs of Central America, births were assisted by a midwife. The umbilical cord of a boy was given to a warrior for burial on a battlefield. That of a girl was buried near the hearth. Chalchiuhtlicue, goddess of fresh water, was especially honored after the birth of a child.

The Aztec water goddess Chalchiuhtlicue was believed to purify a newborn child of the parents' sins. The midwife offered a prayer to her while bathing the newborn to wash away the sins.

A Roman father acknowledges his child by raising the baby in the air.

Growing Up Through History

Children's lives have changed a great deal through history. In the Middle Ages in Europe (about 500 to 1500), many children were abandoned or killed, largely for economic reasons. By the Renaissance (about 1300 to 1600), however, infanticide was condemned by the Catholic Church. In turn, children became more celebrated and were better educated.

This baptismal font from the 1100's was used to baptize babies in orphanages.

This terra-cotta bust of a young boy by Luca della Robbia reflects a changing attitude to children in Renaissance times. Rich families wanted portraits of their children, as they began to give them more love and care.

The celebratory birth tray of a family in Florence shows a mother and newborn child surrounded by a group of female friends and family.

Renaissance Rituals

In the Renaissance period, in France and Italy, women who had just given birth were pampered and given gifts. Beautifully decorated birth trays, commissioned by the father or a close male relative, were especially popular gifts for new mothers in Florence, Italy. The back of the tray often depicted the family coat of arms. The tray was presented to the mother with cookies and small cakes on it. For a short time after the birth, the new mother experienced great honor. A lord's wife might receive a higher allowance, while noblewomen might receive gifts of jewelry, clothes, and land.

Medieval Babies

In the Middle Ages, many parents abandoned their babies for economic reasons. Christian leaders set up the first orphanages to take care of them. In keeping with Christian practices, orphaned babies were baptized to wash away the sins they were thought to possess.

Binding Feet

In ancient China, small feet were considered beautiful. The custom of binding feet to make them smaller began in the 200's B.C. and had become widespread by the A.D. 1100's. Between the ages of 5 and 7, a girl's feet were bound up in cloth. The cloths were tightened until the foot doubled up on itself. The pain was so agonizing that walking was unbearable.

Many Chinese girls suffered the pain of foot-binding. This woman's shoe is only 5 1/4 inches long.

Louis XIII of France reigned from 1610 until 1643. He was crowned king at age 9, but until he came of age, his mother, Marie de Médicis, acted as his regent.

Growing Up To Be King

Many heirs to thrones around the world spent their childhood years preparing for their future role as ruler. Sometimes, as in the case of Louis XIII of France and Edward VI of England and Ireland, they were crowned while still children.

The Biblical story of Herod the Great tells how he celebrated his birthday with a supper for his lords, captains, and other officials.

The First Diploma

Emperor Napoleon I of France (1769–1821) ordered many reforms to French education. In 1808, he created the first high school diploma, known as the Baccalauréat. At age 16, students were examined on all they had been taught at high school, in preparation for attending a university.

Origin of the Birthday Cake

The traditional circular shape of the birthday cake may have come from the ancient Greeks, who offered round cakes to Artemis, goddess of the moon. Or, the birthday cake tradition may have started in Germany hundreds of years ago, when "cake" was actually sweetened bread. The Germans added small surprises to birthday cakes. The object that guests found in their slice supposedly predicted their future. A coin meant wealth, and a thimble meant you would never marry!

A French high school student plays ball in his school uniform in an 1805 engraving.

Birthday Parties Long Ago

Christians have celebrated Christmas, the birthday of Jesus, for about 2,000 years. Other Biblical birthdays include that of one of Egypt's pharaohs (kings), who celebrated his with a feast for members of his court, and Herod the Great, who had a birthday supper. In Europe, the earliest parties were held to protect people from the evil spirits they believed would visit them on their birthday. Friends and family arrived with happy wishes for the celebrant and the coming year. These were thought to ward off any evil spirits. Most guests did not bring gifts, but those who did were considered an especially positive influence on the birthday person.

The ancient Greeks added candles to their birthday cakes to make them look like glowing moons. Some people have believed that smoke from birthday candles takes their wishes up to the gods. Today, people still make silent wishes as they blow out their candles.

LADYBUG BIRTHDAY CAKE

- 2 round 10-inch sponge cakes (store-bought or homemade)
- 1 ½ cups chocolate frosting
- 1 ½ cups vanilla frosting, colored red
- dark colored candy for the spots (such as brown m&m's or round licorice), and brightly colored candy for the eyes and mouth

Cover the top and sides of one cake with chocolate frosting. Cut the other cake in half and cover the tops and sides with the red vanilla frosting. Carefully place the red pieces of cake over the chocolate round so that they look like wings. Decorate with the candy, adding spots, eyes, and a mouth.

THE SONG "HAPPY BIRTHDAY TO YOU" was written by two American sisters, Patty and Mildred Hill, in 1893. The song has been translated into many different languages.

Chinese Traditions

The animals used to decorate children's clothing have special significance. The tiger is a symbol of wealth, and, as king of the forest, is fierce enough to scare off evil spirits.

In traditional Chinese society, pregnant women follow a number of rituals to help ensure that their babies are healthy and happy. Shortly after a baby is born, it is given a name. The name is carefully chosen, because the Chinese believe that the name plays an important role in determining a person's destiny. When the baby is 1 month old, the family holds a special ceremony to celebrate the arrival of a new family member. Friends and relatives give the baby clothes and other presents. In return, the parents give them gifts of food, such as fortune cookies and red-dyed eggs.

Lucky silver charms are given to Chinese babies at their 1-month birthday to help protect them against evil.

The Zhuazhou Ceremony

Traditionally, a child's first birthday is celebrated with a feast and offerings to the gods. The Zhuazhou ceremony also takes place. As friends and relatives watch, the parents sit the baby on the ground, surrounded by a variety of objects, such as toys, pens, and fruit. The object that the baby picks up is said to indicate what the future will bring for him or her.

The Far East

THE FAR EAST

The Far East is the easternmost part of Asia. Asia extends from Africa and Europe in the west to the Pacific Ocean in the east. The northernmost part of the continent is in the Arctic. In the south, Asia ends in the tropics near the equator. Traditionally, the term Far East has referred to China, Japan, North Korea, South Korea, Taiwan, and eastern Siberia in Russia. Southeast Asia includes Borneo, Brunei, Cambodia, East Timor, Indonesia, Laos, Malaysia, Myanmar, the Philippines, Singapore, Thailand, and Vietnam.

Cat shoes were traditionally worn by Chinese children to frighten away evil spirits. The shoes were made from red cotton or silk.

LONG-LIFE NOODLES WITH EGG

- 1 lb. Chinese egg noodles
- ½ lb. frozen spinach, thawed
- 1 cup hot chicken broth
- 1 tablespoon dark soy sauce
- 1 teaspoon sesame oil
- ¼ teaspoon salt
- 1 teaspoon cornstarch dissolved in 1 tablespoon cold water to make paste
- 4 eggs
- 1 tablespoon chives, chopped

Boil noodles in salted water for the time indicated on package. Drain and divide among 4 bowls. Blanch spinach in same water; drain, squeeze, chop. Divide and place in the bowls. Combine the broth with soy sauce, sesame oil, salt, and cornstarch paste. Boil 4 cups of water in a saucepan. Break 4 eggs into the water and poach for 2 minutes. Place 1 egg in each bowl. Pour the hot soup over them. Garnish with chives.

Guardian of Children

The god Chang Hsien is the guardian of children. He protects children and pregnant women from the evil spirit T'ien-Kou Hsing, warding him off with his stringless bow.

In Chinese culture, noodles signify long life and are served on the baby's 1-month birthday and on other special occasions. When eating the noodles, it is considered very unlucky to cut a strand.

Chang Hsien is usually pictured carrying his bow and accompanied by children. Some say that he has a black beard and wears brightly colored robes and a scholar's cap.

Baby's First Haircut

The Chinese believe that shaving a baby's head will leave the baby pure and clean. The hair is usually shaved into a special hairstyle of one or two small tufts or horns. These are intended to fool evil spirits into thinking that the baby is an animal and not worth harming.

Lucky Red Eggs

At a baby's 1-month birthday, many special foods are served and given as gifts. Hard-boiled eggs, dyed red, are particularly important. Red is considered a lucky color, and the shape of the eggs symbolizes a happy and harmonious life.

Buddhist Customs

Chinese Buddhists pray and make offerings to their family ancestors in the hope that they will watch over a child and bring him or her good health and a long life.

Lighting incense sticks is one way Buddhists honor ancestors.

Japanese Celebrations

The ancient religion of Japan is called Shinto, or the way of the gods. Followers worship kami (spirits) believed to live in animals and plants, and in natural places, such as mountains and rivers. Shinto has many rituals that celebrate a baby's birth and his or her passage through childhood. When a baby is about 1 month old, he or she is taken to a shrine for the first time to be blessed by the kami.

Hime-daruma dolls are given to mothers as good luck charms to wish their babies long life and good health.

The Empress Jingu rides on a horse.

7-5-3 Festival
November 15 is the Japanese Shichi-go-san, also called 7-5-3 Festival, for children age 3, for boys age 5, and for girls age 7. Children dress up in their best clothes and visit the shrine for a harai, a purification ceremony intended to remove evil influences from their lives and wish them a happy future. Afterward, each child receives a bag with a lucky charm and candy.

Protector of Children
Hotei is one of the seven Shinto gods of luck. He is the god of happiness and laughter, and the protector of women and children. He is often shown surrounded by children. Legend says that on his back he carries a sack of candy to give to children.

The Stone of Empress Jingu
Legend says that Empress Jingu (A.D. 170–269) set off at the head of a great military expedition to conquer Korea. The empress was pregnant and carried a magic stone on her belly to delay her baby's birth until the campaign was over.

Hotei is the Shinto protector of children.

Coming of Age

In Japan, young people officially become adults at the age of 20. This is when they also are allowed to vote in political elections. An annual coming-of-age ceremony is held on January 15. This national holiday, called Seijin-no-hi, is organized by the city authorities. All those who have turned 20 in the past year visit their local shrine to show their gratitude to the kami and to receive blessings and prayers from the priest.

Clothes for Special Occasions

Although most Japanese people wear Western-style dress, girls still wear traditional kimonos on special occasions, such as the 7-5-3 Festival and the coming-of-age ceremony. Most girls do not own their own kimonos but rent them instead. At the age of 7, girls are allowed to tie their kimono with a wide obi (sash) instead of a cord obi for the first time. For boys, formal dress means haori (half-jackets) and hakama (long, pleated skirts).

A Shinto priest leads the reading of a prayer at a coming-of-age ceremony in Tokyo.

Geta are one type of footwear worn with kimonos. Geta are wooden sandals carved from one piece of wood and fitted with a leather strap. They have thick platform soles for keeping the hem of the kimono off the ground.

Girls dress up in beautiful kimonos for the annual coming-of-age ceremony.

MIKOSHI PROCESSIONS

Mikoshi are portable Shinto shrines paraded through the streets for festivals. It is thought that the kami of a shrine enters the mikoshi and that his or her divine power helps drive evil away. Boys are allowed to carry the main mikoshi to mark their passage into adulthood. Younger boys may carry a smaller one.

A mikoshi is a portable shrine.

Korea and Southeast Asia

This offering in the shape of a baby is made by some people in Indonesia. It is made from rice grains and white thread and is given at a ceremony when the baby is 3 months old.

CONFUCIANISM traditionally has been the most widely followed set of beliefs in Korea. It is more a philosophy than a religion. It stresses the duties that people have toward one another.

In Korea, some women hoping for a son pray to sacred carved stones and rocks.

This father and son are from Mindanao, an island in the southern Philippines.

Most Koreans are Buddhists or Confucianists. In Southeast Asia, people also practice Hinduism, Buddhism, Christianity, Islam, or worship spirits of nature. Each of these religions has its own set of rituals and ceremonies surrounding birth and childhood. In Korea, where family ties are very strong, the birth of a baby is a very special time. After the baby is born, white rice and seaweed soup are served to the mother, to assure her of good health. To thank the spirit of childbirth, the family may place a bowl of water and a bowl of rice in the corner of the birthing room.

Honoring the Spirits

The majority of people living in the Philippines are Roman Catholics. A small percentage are Muslims. In isolated areas, groups of native people still live traditional lifestyles. They worship spirits that live in nature. On special occasions, such as a baby's birth, they honor the spirits and ask for their blessings. Rites of passage in a person's life are often marked by traditional singing and ceremonial dancing.

During the Korean coming-of-age ritual, a boy wears a Confucian hat called a kat for the very first time. The kat is a symbol of adulthood.

Coming of Age

A special ceremony marks a young Korean's coming of age. When girls reach 15, they put their hair up in a bun, fixed in place with a large, ornamental hairpin. When boys become 20 years old, they tie their long hair into a topknot and wear the traditional clothes of an adult.

Birth Rituals in Korea

In traditional Korean society, having a son is very important for carrying on the family name. Korean women pray for a son at sacred sites, such as mountains, rivers, and Buddhist temples. After a baby is born, a rope is hung on a post at the entrance to the house for 21 days. This is thought to help keep strangers and evil influences away.

A monk is ordained in Cambodia.

Buddhist Ordination

In Southeast Asia, many young boys live in a Buddhist monastery as part of their education. Some boys leave the monastery after a few weeks or months. Some, however, go on to become Buddhist monks. Their ordination ceremony is one of the most important events in their life. They put on orange or maroon robes and shave their heads to show that they have cut their ties with the world.

Shinbyu Ceremony

In Myanmar, boys between the ages of 11 and 14 must spend time in a Buddhist monastery. A ceremony called the Shinbyu marks their entrance. The boys dress up as Prince Gautama before he gained enlightenment and became Buddha. Then they exchange these clothes for simple robes. Alms are offered to the boys and monks, and friends and relations are invited to a special meal.

Two boys from **Myanmar** *(formerly Burma) wait for their Shinbyu ceremony. Prince Gautama gave up his luxurious life to live as a simple monk.*

A baby's first bath is a special occasion in Bali.

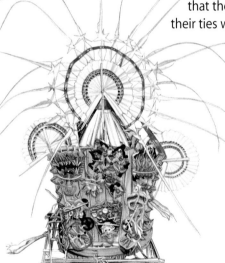

This offering from Bali is dedicated to Ibu Pertiwi, the goddess of the earth.

Birth Rituals in Bali

Many people on the island of Bali, Indonesia, are Hindus. The most important rituals marking a child's birth and early life occur at 12 days, 3 months, and 210 days (one Balinese year) after birth. Offerings are made to thank the gods and ward off evil spirits.

Hill Tribes of Thailand

The forested hills and fertile valleys of northern Thailand are home to a variety of tribes. These tribes live largely traditional lifestyles, following ancient customs and beliefs that have been passed down through generations. The major hill tribes are the Hmong, Karen, Mien, Akha, Lisu, and Lahu. Most of them came originally from China, and their cultural identity is still influenced by Chinese culture. Karen culture, however, has more in common with that of neighboring Myanmar (formerly Burma).

Mien mothers make colorful caps for their babies and young children. The caps are covered in fine appliqué or embroidery and bright red pompons.

Hmong mothers embroider beautifully decorated carrying cloths for their babies.

Hmong Babies

The Hmong believe babies are sent to this world by the baby goddess. At a ceremony held on the third day after a baby's birth, the family sacrifices two chickens to thank the baby goddess and to invite the baby's soul to take its place in the baby's body. The parents then give the baby a name and ask their household spirits to protect it.

A Hmong mother cradles a baby as her other children watch. Family ties are very strong among the hill tribes.

Karen Mothers

A Karen baby is born at home with a relative or midwife helping. Afterward, the mother sits by the fire for three days. To protect the mother and her newborn from evil spirits, an upside-down bamboo basket is placed near the door with a large knife on top. An elder also comes to chant spells over the mother.

The Karen turn over a bamboo basket and put it by the door to protect a mother and her newborn from evil spirits.

A Karen mother wears traditional brass rings to lengthen her neck. Increasing numbers of rings are applied to females' necks from the age of 5.

China's Ethnic Minorities

Most of the hill tribes of northern Thailand migrated from China over a long period. Large numbers of tribal people still live in China, along the Thai border. For centuries these people have lived by growing crops, raising livestock, hunting, and fishing. They have a rich and ancient culture, with their own languages, arts, crafts, legends, and festivals. Although this traditional lifestyle is now threatened by modern influences, China has helped some of its ethnic minorities build homes, villages, and schools and to improve their local economies.

Mien Souls

During pregnancy, Mien believe that a baby's soul lives in places outside the mother's body, such as in the door of the house, the stove, and the rice pounder. The mother gives birth at home. On a selected day after the birth, the baby's name is recorded in the spirit register. This lets the spirits know that another person has arrived in the world. The baby is then taken outside to see the sky.

Akha Spirits

When an Akha baby is born, he or she is not picked up until he or she has cried three times. These cries ask the great spirit, Apoe Miyeh, for three things—his blessing, a soul, and a long life. Then the midwife picks up the baby and gives him or her a temporary name, so that the spirits do not think the baby is unwanted and try to claim the newborn back. A naming ceremony takes place when it is certain that the baby is healthy.

An Akha girl from northern Thailand, left, *wears a traditional headdress covered in beads and silver balls, buttons, and coins.*

A Mien baby wears a pompon cap made by its mother, above. The cloth cap has woolen pompons.

Lisu Naming Rituals

At a Lisu baby's naming ceremony, the family kills a pig. The priest offers some of the pork to the guardian spirit of the village and asks it for a suitable name. After more prayers and offerings, the priest places a bowl of water and two bowls of liquor on a table. He drops a silver coin into the water and then uses two cowrie shells to divine a name. As the Lisu priest calls out names, he drops the cowrie shells into the water. When one lands open side down and the other open side up, the name being called is chosen as the baby's name.

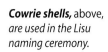

Cowrie shells, above, *are used in the Lisu naming ceremony.*

"Om" is the most sacred sound in Hinduism. *It comes from a Sanskrit word meaning to give life. Hindus believe the universe was created out of this one sound and om continues to be the source of all life.*

South and Central Asia

Hindu Ceremonies

In the Hindu religion, special ceremonies called samskara mark important stages in a person's life. The Sanskrit word *samskara* means purifying or cleansing. Sacred Hindu texts list 16 samskaras, though few people practice them all. The samskaras start before birth and end when a person dies. Many of the ceremonies are performed by a priest in front of a sacred fire.

This mother and baby *are a Hindu temple carving from the 1000's.*

First Samskaras

The first samskaras take place even before a baby is born, to help ensure that the child grows up to be healthy and happy. A pregnant woman reads and recites from the sacred texts so that their words protect her baby. Her husband may part her hair and mark the parting with red powder to protect her from evil spirits. Soon after the baby is born, he or she is bathed, and the sacred word *om* is written on the newborn's tongue in honey.

The great Hindu god Vishnu *is the protector of the universe. During pregnancy, a mother-to-be offers cooked rice to Vishnu to ask for his blessings.*

During the naming ceremony, *the priest gives the parents a metal plate filled with grains of rice. Traditionally, the father writes the baby's name, date of birth, and the name of the family god in the rice grains.*

Naming a Child

About 10 or 12 days after a baby's birth, a priest visits the family to bless and name the child. This is called the Namakarana samskara. The priest advises the parents on a meaningful name, according to the baby's horoscope. Many Hindu babies are named after gods and goddesses.

SOUTH AND CENTRAL ASIA

South and Central Asia are areas of distinct cultures and peoples. These regions form an area at the base of Asia. Asia extends from Africa and Europe in the west to the Pacific Ocean in the east. The northernmost part of the continent is in the Arctic. In the south, Asia ends in the tropics near the equator. South Asia is made up of Afghanistan, Armenia, Bangladesh, Bhutan, India, the Maldives, Nepal, Pakistan, Sri Lanka, the Tibetan plateau in southwest China, and parts of the countries of Azerbaijan and Georgia. Much of India, the largest country in south Asia, forms a peninsula that extends southward into the Indian Ocean. Central Asia includes the countries of Kazakhstan, Kyrgyzstan, Tajikistan, Turkmenistan, Uzbekistan, and the West Siberian Plain.

Childhood Ceremonies

Several samskaras take place as the child grows up. A few months after the naming ceremony, the baby is taken outside for the first time to see the rising sun. When the child is 1 to 3 years old, the child's hair is cut off and burned in the sacred fire. This is done to remove any bad influences and to wish for a good life.

This is the first haircut for this Hindu child.

These pages from the Rig-Veda, the oldest Hindu scripture, are written in Sanskrit, the ancient, sacred language of India.

Ganesh's Blessing

When a Hindu child is about 5 years old and about to start his or her education, the Vidyarambha (beginning of study) samskara is performed. Offerings are made to Ganesh, the god of learning, to bless the child. The child writes the first letter of the alphabet on a tray of uncooked rice.

Ganesh, the elephant-headed Hindu god, is the god of wisdom and the god who solves problems. Hindus pray to Ganesh before they start a new task or journey.

Receiving the Sacred Thread

The Upanayana samskara, also called the Sacred Thread ceremony, is a special occasion in a Hindu boy's life. It is performed when he is between 8 and 12 years old, depending on his caste. It marks the end of his childhood and the start of his adult life. The ceremony takes place in front of a sacred fire. The priest loops the sacred thread over the boy's left shoulder and under his right arm. He must wear it throughout his life.

Studying the Sacred Texts

The Sacred Thread ceremony also marks the beginning of the boy's religious life. He learns the Gayatri Mantra from the Rig-Veda and promises to study the Hindu sacred texts. In the past, boys left home to live and study with a guru (spiritual teacher). Today, they pretend to leave at the end of the Upanayana samskara.

Three cords are twisted together to make the sacred thread around this boy. They represent purity in word, thought, and deed.

Sikh Ceremonies

The Sikhs, who prize family life, welcome babies into the world as precious gifts from God. They hold special ceremonies when a baby is born, when a newborn is given a name, and when a young boy or girl becomes a full member of the Sikh faith. Sikh ceremonies often take place in the gurdwara (house of worship), before a copy of the Guru Granth Sahib, the Sikhs' holy book. After a ceremony, everyone shares karah parshad, a sweet pudding made from sugar, butter, and flour. Sharing food is important for Sikhs, because it demonstrates their belief that everyone is equal in God's eyes.

This Sikh symbol, called the Khanda, is made up of a double-edged sword, which represents the power of God in life and death; a ring of steel symbolizing the unity of God; and two crossed swords that stand for political and spiritual freedom. The Khanda is found on Sikh flags and badges.

A Sikh reader, called a granthi, reads from the Guru Granth Sahib.

Naming Ceremony

A baby's naming ceremony usually takes place at the end of a normal service in the gurdwara. The ceremony is performed in front of the Guru Granth Sahib. The granthi (reader) opens the holy book at random and reads the first verse on the left-hand page. The first letter of the first word is chosen as the first letter of the baby's name. The baby's parents choose a suitable name and tell the granthi, who announces it to the congregation. To show their approval, the congregation replies, "Sat sri akal," which means "Eternal is the great timeless Lord."

First Visit to the Gurdwara

When a baby is born, the words of a Sikh prayer called the Mool Mantra are whispered in its ear. The prayer begins with the words, "There is only one God," a key Sikh belief. A drop of honey may be placed on the baby's tongue to symbolize goodness and purity. Later, the parents take the baby to the gurdwara (house of worship) for the first time, for its naming ceremony. Any building can be a gurdwara, as long as a copy of the Guru Granth Sahib is kept there.

The Golden Temple, called Harimandir (House of God), in Amritsar, India, is the most important gurdwara. It houses a richly jeweled copy of the Guru Granth Sahib.

Joining the Khalsa

The Khalsa is the Sikh brotherhood, begun by Guru Gobind Singh in 1699. Today, many young Sikhs join the Khalsa when they are from 12 to 16 years old. A special ceremony is held in the gurdwara, led by five Sikhs who represent the Panj Piare, the first members of the Khalsa. The people entering the Khalsa bathe and dress in clean clothes including the five K's. They drink amrit (holy water), which is a mixture of sugar and water, as the Panj Piare did.

When Sikhs join the Khalsa, they promise to wear the five K's, as symbols of their faith. These are: kesh (uncut hair); kanga (a comb); kara (a steel bracelet); kirpan (a dagger); and kaccha (under-shorts).

Sikh turbans can be of any color. Normally, older men wear white to symbolize their wisdom. Turbans can also be tied in many different ways.

This illustration shows Guru Gobind Singh and his wife preparing the blessed water used in the initiation ritual.

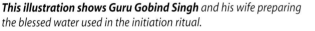

A young Sikh wears a turban with a Khanda badge.

Turban-Tying Ceremony

Sikh men wear turbans as a symbol of their faith and to keep their long hair neat. Sikh men do not believe in cutting their hair. A turban is made of a 15-foot piece of cloth wound around the head. When a boy is about 12 years old, he is taken to the gurdwara, where the granthi or another Sikh elder shows him how to tie his first turban. Friends and relations come to watch the ceremony and to give the boy gifts to mark the special day.

THE 10 GURUS

The Sikh religion began in Punjab, India, about A.D. 1500. Its first great teacher was Guru Nanak (1469–1539). He received a message from God telling him to teach a new religion based on divine love. Guru Nanak was followed by 9 more gurus. Just before the 10th guru, Guru Gobind Singh, died in 1708, he told the Sikhs that their holy book, the Guru Granth Sahib, would serve as their guru from then on.

Guru Nanak, the first Sikh guru, is surrounded by his nine successors.

Being Jewish relates to a religion and not to a country. The children who were placed in this cradle by their Jewish mother in the 1800's in Moravia were just as Jewish as if they had been born in Israel.

The Middle East

Jewish Birth Rituals

The exciting news that a baby is on the way is treated differently, according to whether a Jewish family follows the Ashkenazi or the Sephardic tradition. Ashkenazi Jews have believed that it was best not to share the news with people outside the immediate family until the fourth month of pregnancy. They did not want to tempt evil. In contrast, Sephardic Jews traditionally have celebrated immediately. In both traditions, special prayers are said during pregnancy and childbirth to ensure a healthy baby and an easy birth. At birth, Jewish children are often given an everyday name and a Hebrew name. Ashkenazi Jews usually name a child after a dead relative they wish to honor. Sephardic Jews name their children after living relatives.

Amulets

During pregnancy, Jewish women may focus on their spiritual development to help their unborn child. They say special prayers and may attend study classes. Doing charitable work and giving money to good causes is particularly important. Some pregnant women wear an amulet as protection against misfortune. The amulet usually has God's name inscribed on it.

Naming Ceremonies

In the Reform and Progressive traditions, boys and girls are welcomed into the Jewish community with a naming ceremony at the synagogue. Both parents take part. Orthodox girls are given their name while the father recites a blessing on the first Sabbath after the child's birth. Newborn Orthodox boys are named at their circumcision ceremony.

Judith was a heroine in the Bible. The name Judith is popular among Jews.

Almonds are a symbol of the happy life a pregnant mother wishes for her child.

The Cloth-Cutting Ceremony

Sephardic Jews often celebrate a first pregnancy with a cloth-cutting ceremony. In her fifth month of pregnancy, a mother-to-be invites female friends and relatives to enjoy chocolate, cakes, and sugared almonds. A relative makes a cut in the tablecloth, and the pregnant woman throws sugared almonds onto it to wish her child a sweet and prosperous future.

The Hamsa is a popular amulet to wear during pregnancy. Shaped like the palm of a hand, it is believed to protect the mother and her baby from the evil eye.

JEWISH NAMES

Since the Middle Ages, Jewish people have commonly given their children two names: an everyday name from their culture; and a Hebrew name for religious purposes, usually from the Bible or modern Israel. Here are some common Hebrew boys' names and their meanings:

Binyamin—son of the right hand
Chaim—life
Dan—judge
Yitzhak—he will laugh
Yosef—God will increase

Common Hebrew girls' names and their meanings :

Avigayil—father's joy
Aviva—spring
Elisheva—oath to God
Gavriella—God is my strength
Shoshana—rose or lily

THE MIDDLE EAST

The Middle East covers parts of northern Africa, southwestern Asia, and southeastern Europe. Scholars disagree on which countries make up the Middle East. But many say the region consists of Bahrain, Cyprus, Egypt, Iran, Iraq, Israel, Jordan, Kuwait, Lebanon, Oman, Qatar, Saudi Arabia, Sudan, Syria, Turkey, United Arab Emirates, and Yemen. The region also is the birthplace of three major religions—Judaism, Christianity, and Islam.

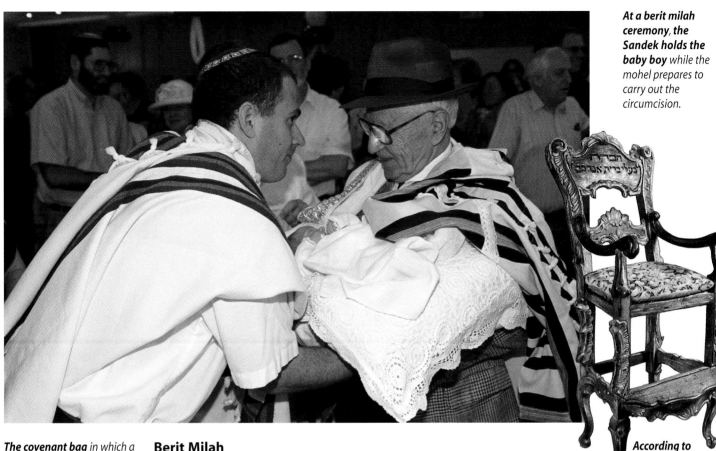

At a berit milah ceremony, the Sandek holds the baby boy while the mohel prepares to carry out the circumcision.

According to Jewish custom, a chair for Elijah the Prophet is positioned to the right of the Sandek's chair at circumcisions.

The covenant bag in which a baby is carried to its naming ceremony is kept as a souvenir. It is later used at the child's bar or bat mitzvah.

Berit Milah

Circumcision is a ritual that marks the entry of a Jewish boy into the covenant (bond) between God and the Jewish people. The ceremony occurs when the baby is 8 days old. The godfather carries the baby, lying on a cushion, into the room. He is then held by the Sandek during the ceremony. It is an honor to be chosen as the Sandek, the person who holds the baby. The father recites a blessing. Next, a trained person called a mohel cuts the foreskin off the baby's penis. (The procedure is very quick, and the penis heals in a few days.) The mohel blesses and names the baby. A festive meal follows.

This girl from the country Georgia is wearing traditional Sephardic clothing.

The Covenant Bag

Jewish people wear special garments for prayer. The covenant bag is a velvet bag used to carry a baby boy to his berit milah or a baby girl to her naming ceremony. Some Sephardic Jews name their daughters at a ceremony called zeved habat (the gift of a daughter) when she is 14 or 66 days old. The rabbi blesses the baby, and there is a celebration meal. Nowadays, many parents perform a new ritual, called simhat bat. Blessings are recited, and the baby is given her Jewish name.

TWO TRADITIONS

After the Jews were defeated by the Romans in A.D. 70, they dispersed all over the world. They continued to move whenever they were persecuted. Between the 900's and 1200's, two main groups of Jews formed. The Sephardim were forced to leave Spain in 1492 and moved to countries under Muslim rule. The Ashkenazim spread eastward from Germany into Eastern Europe. The Sephardim adopted their own Jewish language, Ladino, and the Ashkenazim developed Yiddish. Gradually, differences between the two groups have become less distinct.

Jewish Rites of Passage

The Torah scrolls are protected by a mantle. At their bar or bat mitzvah, a boy or girl reads from the Torah in synagogue for the very first time.

The key events in a Jewish person's life are marked by rituals. Shortly after birth, a boy is circumcised and a girl has her naming ceremony. At the age of 3, children begin their formal Jewish education. A boy is given a prayer shawl and begins to wear a skullcap. When a girl is 12 or 13, she becomes bat mitzvah; a 13-year-old boy becomes bar mitzvah. This means they become full adult members of the community. Bat and bar mitzvah ceremonies mark the occasion.

Clothing for prayer includes the tallit (prayer shawl) and the tefillin (small leather boxes).

Prayer

Jewish people say set prayers at regular times and pray when they choose. Once a boy becomes bar mitzvah, he wears a prayer shawl called a tallit for normal morning prayers. The tallit is made of white cloth with blue or black stripes and fringes called tsitsit. Two small black boxes called tefillin, which contain Bible passages, are wrapped around his arms. On his head, he wears a skullcap called a yarmulka or kippah. Out of modesty, women may also cover their heads to pray.

The Western Wall, right, is a Jewish holy place in Jerusalem. It is a popular site for a bar mitzvah.

THE SYNAGOGUE

A synagogue is a Jewish community center, where people pray and study. Most religious ceremonies take place there. At the front of the synagogue is the Ark, which safely holds the Torah scrolls. The scrolls are the holiest objects in the synagogue. The Torah is read from the bimah, a raised platform in the middle of the room.

The Ten Commandments

The term *bar mitzvah* means son of the commandments, and *bat mitzvah* means daughter of the commandments. Once young people have gone through this important rite of passage, they are responsible for following all the Jewish laws. For example, the Ten Commandments instruct Jewish people to recognize one God, keep the Sabbath, respect their parents, and not kill, steal, or desire anything that is not theirs.

The Tablets of the Law, inscribed with the Ten Commandments, are kept at the front of the synagogue.

Adulthood

According to Jewish tradition, girls reach adulthood at age 12 or 13, and boys at age 13. To commemorate this, girls have a bat mitzvah ceremony and boys have a bar mitzvah. On the Sabbath after his birthday, a boy is called up to read the Torah in synagogue for the first time. Now that they are considered adults, these boys and girls must observe all the Jewish laws and be responsible for their actions. This includes observing all holy days. owadays, the bat mitzvah ceremony is little different from a bar mitzvah.

Girls in Orthodox Communities usually have their bat mitzvah together in small groups.

A Party to Celebrate

Following a bar or bat mitzvah ceremony, the family usually throws a huge party for family and friends, with plenty of food, dancing, and singing. The party may begin with Kiddush, the blessing said over wine. During the meal, friends and relatives make speeches to encourage the young person to take pleasure in his or her new role as a Jewish adult. The young person receives presents, some of which are religious items, others tailored to his or her interests. But the focus of the day is the ceremony in the synagogue, not the festivities that follow.

A lavish dinner is offered to guests after a bar or bat mitzvah ceremony.

Islamic Birth Ceremonies and Rites of Passage

This decorative tile from the Ottoman Empire in the 1800's is inscribed with the words ma sha'a Allah (what Allah wills) which expresses the idea that all good comes from God.

For Muslims, Islam is the acceptance of the will of the one true God, called Allah in Arabic. Muslims are guided by their holy book, the Quran. The Middle East is the historical center of the Islamic world, but most Muslims live in south and southeastern Asia. Also, many live in North Africa. Muslims view the family as the basis for society. New babies are welcomed into the community as soon as they are born. Various rituals accompany a child's journey to adulthood and are part of his or her Islamic education.

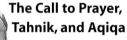

Traditionally, an animal such as a goat or sheep is sacrificed in thanksgiving for the gift of a child.

The Call to Prayer, Tahnik, and Aqiqa

Just after a child's birth, the head of the family whispers the call to prayer into the baby's ears. Also shortly after a child's birth, a tiny piece of sugar, chewed date, or honey is rubbed into the baby's mouth. The oldest and most respected member of the family has the honor of doing this ritual, called the tahnik. It is supposed to encourage the baby to suckle. It also is a symbol to make the baby "sweet"—kind and obedient. Prayers for the baby and family follow. Seven days after birth, friends and relatives enjoy a festive ceremony called Aqiqa, when the baby is named. Later, boys are circumcised—the foreskin is cut from their penis. This is done while they are babies or sometime later but before age 13, depending on the country.

At Aqiqa, the baby's head is shaved, and the weight of the shaved hair in gold or silver is given to the poor.

Coming of Age

From the age of about 7, Muslim children start to learn their role in society. Boys begin to attend prayers in the mosque with their father, while girls learn to pray at home. In some parts of the world, a Muslim girl starts to wear long clothes and cover her head at puberty. In some places, families celebrate when a girl begins to wear a veil to cover her face.

Learning about Islam

Some Muslims hold a Bismillah (also spelled Basmala) ceremony when the child begins to speak and can learn the first lesson from the Quran by heart and how to pray. When they are a little older, children—whatever their mother tongue—learn Arabic so that they can read the Quran. Once children are about 12, they are considered adults and are expected to carry out all Muslim practices. At any age from 15 upward, Muslims may declare their faith by reciting the shahada (an act of bearing witness). They publicly recite the shahada and thus officially join the Muslim religious community.

These boys at a Muslim school *in Pakistan are learning to read the Quran. Arabic is the language of Islamic worship.*

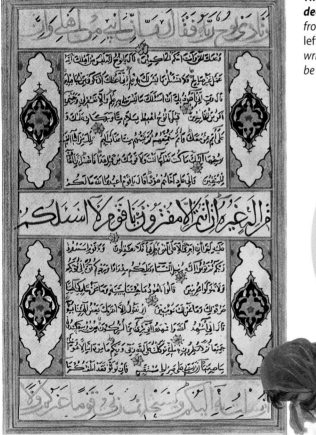

This beautifully decorated page *from the Quran, left, shows that written Arabic can be an art in itself.*

The words of the shahada *form the image of a man at prayer in a Moroccan panel. The words are "I bear witness that there is no God but Allah. I bear witness that Muhammad is the Messenger of Allah."*

Lentil soup *is sometimes made to break fast during Ramadan.*

LENTIL SOUP—MAKHLOUTA

- 1 cup dried lentils
- 1 cup dried garbanzo beans
- 1 cup dried black beans
- 1 teaspoon salt
- 1 cup rice
- ½ cup finely chopped onions
- ½ teaspoon caraway seeds
- ¼ cup extra-virgin olive oil
- 6–8 cups water

Soak the lentils and garbanzo and black beans overnight in enough cold water to cover. Place in a large, heavy-bottomed saucepan with the water and cook for about 1 hour, or until tender. Season with salt when almost done. Cook the rice separately and add to the bean mixture when tender. Brown the onions with the caraway seeds in the oil and add to the rice and beans. Pour in 6 to 8 cups water and simmer over low heat until the soup is thick and ready to serve.

THE FIVE PILLARS OF ISLAM

Muslim children learn to follow five basic practices, called the Five Pillars of Islam. They are taught to recite the shahada and to pray five times a day. As they grow older, they join in the fast from dawn to sunset each day of Ramadan, an Islamic holy month. They give money to charity (a practice called zakah), and once in their lifetime they go on hajj, the pilgrimage to Mecca.

Muslims face *toward Mecca when they say their prayers.*

Christian Rites of Passage

Christianity, which is the dominant religion in Europe and the Americas, was divided in the A.D. 1000's to form the Orthodox Churches in the East and the Roman Catholic Church in the West. The Western Church was further divided following the Reformation in the 1500's, when Protestantism was founded. Since then, Protestantism has divided into many branches as various groups interpreted the teachings of Jesus in different ways. In spite of these divisions, the major Christian churches believe sacraments are a way of bestowing God's blessing on his followers. The most important of these to children are baptism, the Eucharist, and confirmation.

Most Christians believe in the Trinity, in which God is the Father, the Son, and the Holy Spirit. The Holy Spirit guides them throughout their lives and is symbolized by a dove, above.

Most Christians are baptized by having holy water poured over their forehead when they are babies. In adult baptism, a person may be totally immersed in water, symbolizing the washing away of his or her old life.

Europe and the Americas

Baptism

The sacrament of baptism admits people into the Christian faith and makes them part of the Christian community. It also purifies them from sin, allowing them to start a new life in Jesus. The Roman Catholic Church and many Protestant churches baptize people as babies. During the baptism ceremony, godparents make promises on behalf of the child, who also receives a name during the ceremony. However, some Protestant churches baptize people only as adults, when they are able to understand the concepts of sin and forgiveness.

EUROPE

Europe is one of the smallest of the world's seven continents in area but one of the largest in population. Europe extends from the Arctic Ocean in the north to the Mediterranean Sea in the south and from the Atlantic Ocean in the west to the Ural Mountains in the east. The 47 countries of Europe include the world's largest country, Russia, as well as the world's smallest, Vatican City. Russia lies partly in Europe and partly in Asia.

JESUS'S BAPTISM

Jesus himself was baptized, by His cousin John the Baptist around A.D. 27. Christians believe that this baptism marked the beginning of Jesus's public ministry. Once cleansed of His own sin, He was prepared to save others from their sins, renew their lives, and lead them into the Kingdom of God.

Jesus being baptized by John the Baptist.

In the celebration of the Eucharist, *the bread, known as the host, may be in the form of a wafer,* left, *or a small loaf,* above.

Members of some Protestant churches *do not drink alcohol. For communion, they have a nonalcoholic drink instead of wine.*

Roman Catholic girls dress all in white, *like miniature brides, for their First Holy Communion, which typically takes place around age 7.*

The Eucharist or Mass

The sacrament of the Eucharist or Mass is a celebration of the Last Supper, which Jesus ate with His disciples shortly before He was arrested and crucified. The Eucharist is also known as Holy Communion and is accepted in various forms by nearly all Christians on Saturdays or Sundays and on holy days of obligation. In the celebration, the priest or minister blesses bread and wine, which is then shared among the congregation. Protestants believe that the bread and wine represent the body and blood of Jesus, but Eastern Orthodox Christians and Roman Catholics believe that the bread and wine turn into Jesus's actual body and blood after they are blessed.

Through the act of penance, above, *Eastern Orthodox Christians and Roman Catholics believe Jesus forgives those who are sorry for their sins. Starting at about age 9, children take responsibility for their actions and accept the sacrament of penance for their misdeeds.*

Confirmation

At their confirmation ceremony, young Christians become full members of the church by confirming the promises that were made for them at their baptism. Roman Catholics are confirmed, and thus strengthened by the Holy Spirit, a few years after their first Holy Communion. Most Protestants are confirmed in their early teens. In the Orthodox Churches, baptism, confirmation, and the first Eucharist all take place at the same time. The infant is immersed in water three times and then anointed with Holy Chrism (oil).

Many Christians confirm their belief *in God to a bishop.*

Graduates typically wear mortarboards (graduation caps) with tassels to accept their diplomas, which are sometimes rolled and tied with ribbons. Graduation from a college or university and the start of a working life is the final step into adulthood for a growing number of people in Europe and the Americas.

STARTING SCHOOL IS AN IMPORTANT STEP a child takes toward growing up. In Ukraine, parents dress their children in fancy clothes and give them flowers on their first day of school.

THE AMERICAS

The continents of North America and South America make up the Western Hemisphere. North America contains Canada, Greenland, the United States, Mexico, Central America, and the Caribbean Sea islands. South America contains Argentina, Bolivia, Brazil (which occupies almost half the continent), Chile, Colombia, Ecuador, Guyana, Paraguay, Peru, Suriname, Uruguay, and Venezuela.

Quinceañera and Nonreligious Rituals

Europe and the Americas have people of many different religions as well as people with no religion at all. As a result, not everyone follows Christian rites of passage. No matter what they believe, however, everyone celebrates birth and growing up in some way. Some ceremonies, such as the school prom, are quite formal. But others, such as baby showers given for expectant mothers, can be very relaxed. Other signs of growing up include becoming eligible to vote in political elections and learning to drive a car.

Quinceañera

Mexicans and other Hispanics celebrate a girl's coming of age on her 15th birthday with a Quinceañera. For this, the girl is dressed in a long gown, with gloves, a tiara, and a bouquet. Friends and family bring gifts to church at a special birthday mass. The girl has an escort and is followed by 14 couples. Each couple represents one year of her life. Her parents accompany her, too. After the mass, there is a big party with traditional food, music, and dancing.

*At **Quinceañera**, a girl enters church with her family and friends for a special mass said in her honor. During the ceremony, the priest talks about the responsibilities of adulthood.*

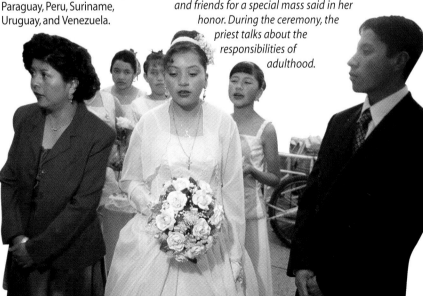

A baby shower is held several weeks before the baby is due.

Baby Showers

Baby showers are very popular in the United States. They are organized by close friends or family and all the guests bring gifts for the expected child. Babies are attracted by things that move. That makes mobiles popular gifts. Traditionally, showers were female-only events and were held for only the first child. But now, men are often invited, and there may be a shower for every child.

MAKE A MOBILE FOR A BABY

• 2 wire hoops: one 12 inches in diameter, one 6 inches in diameter
• scissors
• glue
• colored ribbon or crepe paper
• colored paper
• stiff cardboard
• fine string or nylon yarn

1. Twist 2 different colored ribbons around each hoop to make stripes. Glue in the loose ends.
2. Cut animal shapes from colored paper. Glue them onto cardboard. When dry, cut out the shapes and paint the reverse side to match the ribbons.
3. Attach the 2 hoops with 4 lengths of ribbon, 2 in each color, so that the small hoop hangs above the large one.
4. Make a hole at the top of each animal and thread it with string or yarn. Tie the animals at equal distances but different lengths around the large hoop.
5. Make a loop with one of the colored ribbons and attach it to the smaller hoop.

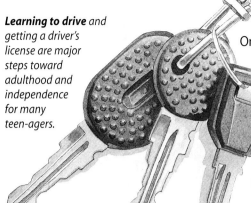

Learning to drive and *getting a driver's license are major steps toward adulthood and independence for many teen-agers.*

New Status

One sign of increasing maturity is when boys and girls start dating. High school Senior Prom is a particularly important date night for some students. Prom is a school dance at which many girls wear their first formal dress and high-heeled shoes. The boys are dressed in suits and dress shoes, rather than jeans and sneakers. Some people say going to a prom is like a test-run for one's wedding.

Getting a first pair of high-heeled shoes makes many girls start to feel grownup.

Voting

Becoming an adult gives a person more civil rights. One of the most important of these is the right to vote in elections for both local and national officials. In most countries, the voting age was changed from 21 to 18 during the 1970's.

An 18-year-old in the United States studies a list of candidates before casting his first vote.

Graduation

Graduation from high school, college, or university is marked by a special ceremony in many countries, particularly in the United States. Many students buy school rings with their class insignia to wear on the third finger of their right hand. They also buy a school year book with photographs of everyone in the class and information about them. The graduation ceremony itself is solemn, with the graduates wearing formal attire and special caps and gowns to receive their diplomas. It is followed by a carefree celebration.

On graduation day, classmates and friends congratulate one another after the ceremony, left. Graduation marks the successful completion of many years of hard study.

American Indians

For thousands of years, North America was populated by many different groups of people whom we now call American Indians. They had different ways of life, depending on where they lived. For example, those who lived along the coast fished, while those on the Great Plains hunted buffalo. In other areas, American Indians had small farms where they grew just enough to feed themselves. But they all shared a life that was in harmony with the world about them.

Many American Indian traditions were lost after Europeans began settling in North America.

This Pomo basket, decorated with feathers and shells, comes from a set of four used by a Pomo girl at her puberty ceremony. The Pomo people from California used baskets for both practical and ceremonial purposes. The baskets were woven by the women from roots, ferns, and willow.

This double amulet contains the umbilical cords of Crow twins. It was tied to their cradle to protect them and wish them long life.

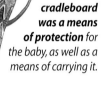

The cradleboard was a means of protection for the baby, as well as a means of carrying it.

Birth Rituals

American Indians see the birth of a child as a happy event, though different groups practice different birth rituals. Some smear the new baby with buffalo fat, while others rub it with soft animal skins or moss before lacing it into a cradleboard. The birth is often celebrated with a feast at which the child is named. This name is not fixed for life, however, and might be changed several times.

This deerskin robe is decorated with beads and shells and was made for a Cheyenne woman around 1870, when the Cheyenne were living on the northern plains.

Cheyenne Society

Among the Cheyenne, who esteemed women highly, a girl's first menstrual period was a cause for celebration. If her father was rich, he marked the occasion by giving away a horse. Meanwhile, the girl bathed and was covered in red paint by the older women before being purified by the smoke from a special fire. Then, wearing her mother's best robe, she spent four days in the menstrual hut with her grandmother, learning about her rights and duties as a woman.

POWWOW

During powwows, American Indians from different groups come together to dance, sing, and celebrate their rich heritage. It is a time for remembering the ancestors who have lost their lives in the struggle to keep their identity. It is also a time for meeting new people from other groups, and for having fun. The powwow begins with a parade of people carrying their group flags followed by the chiefs, elders, and dancers in colorful clothing. The dance performances are the highlight of the powwow.

MANY AMERICAN INDIAN RITUALS were banned by the U.S. government in the early 1900's, but the American Indian Religious Freedom Act of 1978 allowed them to continue.

This American Indian boy entertains an audience with the hoop dance at a powwow.

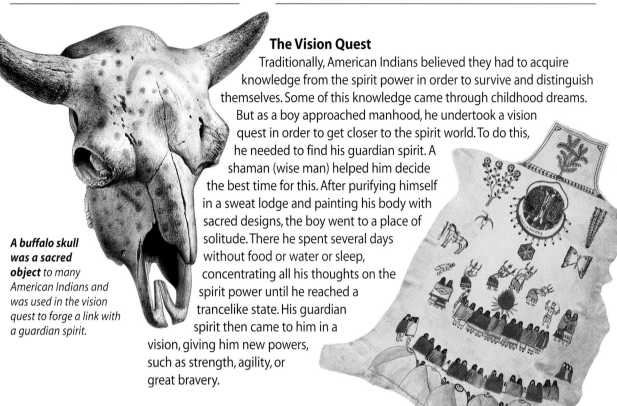

A buffalo skull was a sacred object to many American Indians and was used in the vision quest to forge a link with a guardian spirit.

The Vision Quest

Traditionally, American Indians believed they had to acquire knowledge from the spirit power in order to survive and distinguish themselves. Some of this knowledge came through childhood dreams. But as a boy approached manhood, he undertook a vision quest in order to get closer to the spirit world. To do this, he needed to find his guardian spirit. A shaman (wise man) helped him decide the best time for this. After purifying himself in a sweat lodge and painting his body with sacred designs, the boy went to a place of solitude. There he spent several days without food or water or sleep, concentrating all his thoughts on the spirit power until he reached a trancelike state. His guardian spirit then came to him in a vision, giving him new powers, such as strength, agility, or great bravery.

The Sunrise Ceremony

The Apache mark a girl's initiation into womanhood with the four-day Sunrise Ceremony to give her the spirit and characteristics of the White Painted Woman. The girl's skin is painted with clay and sprinkled with yellow cattail pollen, which she must wear throughout the ceremony, and she dresses in a special doeskin robe. During the ceremony, songs and chants are performed, and the girl spends many exhausting hours dancing, running, and praying. On the last night, she dances from sunset to sunrise for the welfare of the group.

The picture on this doeskin shows Apache dancers taking part in a Sunrise Ceremony in the 1890's, when many American Indian traditions were in danger of being lost forever.

WHITE PAINTED WOMAN IS THE SELF-RENEWING GODDESS. She is always able to make herself young again. The Apache believe that every time she begins to look old, she walks east until she merges with her young self coming toward her. Apaches regard her as their great Earth mother.

An older woman, or godmother, is chosen by the family as a role model for the girl. The godmother accompanies the girl throughout the four-day ceremony and gives advice and teaches the girl about the duties of womanhood.

Celebrating Babies in Africa

Across the vast continent of Africa, the birth of a child is celebrated in different ways and at different times. In some societies, ceremonies begin as soon as the baby is born. But in many, they begin after a few days. This may be partly because some traditions say that it takes a while for the baby's spirit to leave the world of the ancestors and enter this one. Also, life in much of Africa frequently has been harsh. Many babies have died soon after birth. So many African cultures traditionally delayed a birth announcement or ceremony until it appeared the baby would live. Then the child was introduced to the rest of the family and became part of the community.

This fertility doll from Cameroon in West Africa is made from a ripe corncob, threaded corn beads, and plant fibers. Fertility dolls are hoped to ensure women give birth to many healthy children.

This Turkana doll is made out of three palm nuts that stuck together as they grew.

Africa

Precious Dolls

Like other girls across the world, African girls love to play with dolls. But dolls in many African communities are also used to teach girls how to look after babies and toddlers. In some Angolan societies, dolls are treated like children. Adult women make the dolls and give them to the girls in their family. The Ashanti from Ghana make carved wooden Akua'ba dolls. Girls and young women carry these to ensure fertility.

AFRICAN NAMES AND THEIR MEANINGS

Girls' names and their meanings:

Chiku—chatterer
Ebun—gift
Hiwot—life
Makena—the happy one, happiness
Nadra—unusual
Safia—pure and wise
Sekai—laughter
Yasumini—friendliness, sweetness
Zena—news or fame

Boys' names and their meanings:

Adwin—artist or thinker
Ghe'le—strength
Jafari—creek
Kashka—friendly
Mani—from the mountain
Matata—troublemaker
Popota—talkative, shouter
Rafiki—friend
Tumo—fame

The heads of Akua'ba dolls are flat, which is considered very beautiful. Traditionally, pregnant mothers carried a doll with a round head if she wanted a girl, a doll with a square head if she wanted a boy.

Naming the Baby

In parts of Africa, a baby is sometimes named after what happened at the time of its birth. For instance, if there was a storm, the baby might be given a name that means storm. In a naming tradition of Luo people of East Africa, the family examines the baby to determine if it looks or behaves like any ancestors. The chosen ancestors' names are then called out while the baby is crying. The baby is named after the ancestor whose name is being called when the baby stops crying.

AFRICA

Africa lies south of Europe and west of Asia and contains 53 independent countries. Tropical rain forests dominate western and central Africa. The world's largest desert, the Sahara, stretches across northern Africa. Africa also has the world's longest river—the Nile. Much of the continent is grassland. In the north, most of the people are Arabs. The great majority of the African population lives south of the Sahara.

In a West African Yoruba naming ceremony, the baby tastes or touches different foods and objects. These are symbols of life, health, wealth, and happiness. Cola nuts, right, represent medicine. During the ceremony, people pray that the nuts will be used wisely by the child.

The Elders' Choice

Among the Maasai of Kenya, a baby's birth is honored by slaughtering a goat, which is cooked and eaten at a feast. Then the mother and baby have their heads shaved. On the night of the naming ceremony, the mother and baby go outside to milk a goat. When they return, the father and three family elders tell the baby and the mother the name they have chosen.

Among the Maasai, right, and many other Africans, motherhood is seen as women's main role.

A Double Celebration!

In many parts of West Africa, twins are seen as a great blessing. And people believe twins have more spiritual powers than a single baby. Thus, there are special ceremonies for twins. In many communities, each twin is given a little salt and palm oil to taste shortly after birth. This stops any spirits brought by the twins from harming anyone. Twins may also be given special names. Among the Bali of Cameroon, a boy twin is called Sama and a girl twin Nah. In many societies, a doll is made if one twin dies. The doll is dressed and looked after with great care.

TO SHOW THAT SHE HAS GIVEN BIRTH TO HER FIRST SON, a Rendille woman from north-central Kenya builds her hair into a mound with mud, animal fat, and ochre.

The Fon people of Benin make two dolls called Hovi if both twins die.

The Himba's Greatest Blessing

The Himba of Namibia in southern Africa carry their precious babies everywhere. They never leave them alone or put them down. This protects the babies from dangerous animals and from wandering off into the grasslands. It also protects them from harmful spirits who the Himba believe live in the wild countryside. Himba families herd cattle and goats, taking them from one pasture to another. It is very important to keep babies safe as they travel.

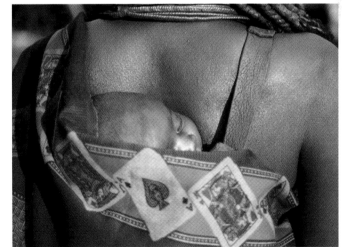

A Himba baby rides on his mother's back. Himba babies go everywhere with their mothers.

CREATIVE TWINS

Twins are very special to the Fon people of Benin in West Africa. According to Fon legend, twin gods created the universe. Mawu, the beautiful goddess of the moon, used her wisdom to fashion the heavens and Earth. She was helped by Lisa, the god of the sun. Mawu wears a crescent moon headdress and a shawl like the night sky.

Simple, carved figures of Mawu and Lisa spread their arms around the world, which is held together by a coiled snake.

Boys Coming of Age in Africa

Every region of Africa has its own way of preparing boys and young men for adulthood. In many communities, boys of a particular age group are taken to a wild part of the countryside. There, they learn how to survive without adults. They also learn how to get along with each other in a mature way. The boys, or initiates, then take part in initiation rituals and celebrations.

This is a patterned Kikuyu initiation shield from Kenya. A Kikuyu boy will hold a shield like this in an initiation dance, to imitate the warrior that he will become. The patterns are etched for each initiation ceremony and then smoothed out again before a new one begins.

These two teen-age boys are age mates who went through circumcision rituals together. After the ordeal, they paint patterns on each other's faces.

A Maasai warrior's most important test is to stalk and kill a lion. The lion's mane is worn as a headdress on ceremonial occasions, below.

Owo men wear ceremonial swords to symbolize their status in society. This ivory sword once belonged to a high-ranking leader. The figure on the blade represents the person carrying the sword, while the intricate carving indicates his high-ranking position.

Secret Societies

In many parts of West Africa, boys who are about to become adults enter secret societies. The boys become members by completing initiation rituals, often in secret, sacred places. One of these rituals is a ceremonial death that symbolizes leaving childhood behind. In the Yoruba Oro society, a ram is slaughtered as part of the initiation. Because rams symbolize manhood, the boys drink the ram's blood.

Becoming a Warrior

In some East African societies, teen-agers take part in many rituals and tests before they can become a warrior. For the Maasai, boys first have to be circumcised. Circumcision in many African societies is an act of bravery and an offering to gods and spirits. It is also considered an act of cleansing.

Taneka initiates wear a buffalo horn headdress *called a Biri, which is painted for the occasion. The successful initiate gives his sister the Biri to wear as a trophy.*

The Dance of the Taneka

Dance and mime are an important part of many African initiation rituals. Taneka initiates from northern Benin in West Africa are known as Sana. The Sana perform dances in front of elders for several days before they are circumcised. The Sana wear two freshly woven white cloths as a symbol of purity for the first few energetic dances. The last dance before circumcision is the Ngani. Musicians accompany the Ngani with drums and iron bells. This time, the initiates have their hair shaved into intricate patterns. They wear a headdress of white feathers bound to red bamboo quills.

The head teacher among the Jokwe of Angola is known as the father of masks. He wears this pointed mask, called a Cikunza mask, and leads the ceremonial initiation rituals.

DANCING WITH MASKS
Lwalwa initiates of Congo (Kinshasa) in central Africa wear wooden masks as they dance. A string is threaded through holes between the lips and nose of the mask. It is then gripped tightly between the initiate's teeth to keep the mask from slipping.

Learning Behind a Mask

In many parts of Africa, initiates and their teachers both wear masks. Masks help an initiate to concentrate on getting rid of his childlike ways. He emerges from the mask as a different, more mature person. Jokwe initiates from Angola are taught how to behave as adults by masked teachers. The teachers' masks are made from bark, twigs, cloth, and tree gums. They are decorated with symbols. The masks represent all the spirits of the universe, led by the Mukishi, a very powerful being. The teachers take the initiates far into the countryside to help them through their initiation classes.

Carved wooden masks *like this one are worn by Lwalwa youths of central Africa during their initiation into manhood.*

These Bassari masked dancers represent spirits from the sacred forest. They challenge the initiates to a symbolic combat. The boys must fight to show they are brave and strong.

The Legend of the Chameleon

The Bassari people live in the hills of Senegal and Guinea in West Africa. Young Bassari initiates are known as Koré. They are between 15 and 20 years old. It takes several months for them to pass their initiation rituals. Older initiates take the Koré away from the village to live separately for a while. Initiation begins in a nearby sacred forest. Here, it is said, the Koré are eaten by Numba, a chameleon god. Numba spits them out again as young adults. After circumcision, the Koré take part in hunting trips. Hunting is part of the Bassari culture and economy.

Girls Coming of Age in Africa

In many parts of Africa, girls begin training for adulthood between the ages of 8 and 12, depending on when they begin menstruating. They usually begin training in a private place away from the community. There, the girls learn crafts and household skills such as cooking and hygiene. More importantly, they learn the ancient customs, rituals, and traditions of their community. Proper initiation turns young girls into wise women who will keep their culture alive. After they have studied, passed tests, and taken part in rituals, young girls leave childhood and become women. Now these initiates can dress in beautiful costumes and share their success with their community by dancing and singing.

This Duma mask from southern Gabon in central Africa represents the guardian spirit of initiation for teen-age girls. The face is whitened with fine white clay called kaolin.

This ceremonial initiation helmet represents the ancestors who watch over the initiate. Small features, a high forehead, and hair braided in intricate patterns are considered signs of the perfect Sande woman.

Secret Societies

In some parts of Africa, girls are initiated into womanhood through different kinds of secret societies. One of these societies is Sande. Sande is an organization of women from several cultures in Guinea, Sierra Leone, and Liberia. Members of the society teach the girls child care, farming, and medicine. When the girls have finished their initiation, they perform a celebration dance. They dress from head to foot in black gowns and wear wooden masks. Wooden masks are usually worn only by men in other parts of Africa.

Successful Krobo initiates take part in an all-night girls' dance in front of their community. Each dancing girl wears a headdress called a cheia. It is made of black cord wound around hoops of cane.

Dipo Rites of the Krobo

Krobo and Shai girls from eastern Ghana are taken away on a three-week course of initiation. The initiation is known as Dipo, and it is blessed by the earth goddess, Nene Kloweki. Ritual mothers put the girls on a diet of traditional food and dress them in red cloths and red carnelian beads. They shave each girl's head, except for a small tuft that is removed after initiation. Then the girls are bathed. These rituals mark the end of childhood. The "mothers" then teach the girls household skills and how to behave and dress well. Finally the girls are worthy of a blessing by the priest and by the spirit of a ritual stone called Tekpete.

The Dance of Success

Senufo girls from the Ivory Coast in West Africa begin their initiation when they are 8 years old. Initiation lasts for seven years. Ritual mothers teach the girls secret rituals, household skills, and pride in womanhood. Women are very strong and have great influence in Senufo communities. The girls also take part in a celebration dance called the Ngoron. Learning the Ngoron's difficult steps and moves can take six months. Like many initiation dances and celebrations, the Ngoron is meant to honor the gods and spirits of women's initiation. It is also a way of including the rest of the community in their initiation. The dancers wear headdresses and necklaces made of cowrie shells, which are a symbol of female beauty. The shells, which were once used as money in parts of Africa, also represent wealth.

These Senufo initiates are admiring one another's cowrie headdresses before the Ngoron dance begins.

Young Bassari initiates wear beadwork clothes and jewelry. The amount of beadwork and the style show which age group they belong to. Older women wear more intricate designs.

Bassari Beadwork

Bassari girls live in the hills of Guinea and Senegal in West Africa. Bassari women are organized into eight age grades. Every six years, they take part in initiation rituals to move up to the next grade. Initiation begins at the age of 12, when girls become young women. But the most important ceremony is Ohamona, which takes place when women are 35. At this age, they are trained to organize community work and to supervise age-grade rituals.

This portion of a beadwork belt, above, *was made and worn by a young Zulu girl from South Africa. The patterns and colors show where the artist comes from and whether she is married. The colors used for love charms show different emotions.*

This small initiation doll, right, *has a beaded apron and hoops around its legs. The hoops represent rolls of body fat, which are seen as a sign of beauty.*

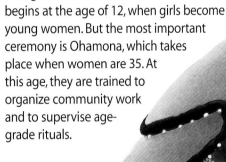

Ndebele beadwork, once mostly white, now features colored motifs, below. *Colors and patterns depend on the latest fashion.*

Ndebele Womanhood

Ndebele initiates from South Africa spend three months being taught beadwork, painting, household skills, and other Ndebele customs. The successful initiates parade through the streets wearing patterned beaded aprons and thick hoops around their legs. Before initiation, young girls wear an igabe. This is made of matching beaded hoops around the waist and beaded tassels attached to it. During initiation, girls wear isiphephetu, which is a stiff apron worn at the front. When they have passed all their tests, young women are allowed to put on a plain, long, soft leather apron called an isithimba. The women are allowed to add beaded patterns as they get older and gain respect.

During initiation ceremonies bull-roarers *are swung in the air over the head. The sound they produce is considered to be a spirit voice. They are kept hidden and used only for special ceremonies.*

Australasia and Oceania

Rites and Rituals

Traditionally, the native people of Australasia and Oceania lived in close harmony with the land, getting most of their food by hunting or fishing and gathering wild plants. It was often a hard life in which they had to be both brave and strong in order to survive. Because of this, many of the boys had to undergo long and painful initiation ceremonies before they could become full members of their tribes. Girls and women had their own rituals, usually on a much smaller scale. For both sexes, the ceremonies marked the passage from childhood to adulthood and helped them bond to their environment.

This Aboriginal painting of a pregnant woman *was painted in X-ray style. This style of painting shows the outside of the body, such as fingers and eyes, as well as internal parts, such as bones, veins, and her unborn child.*

Women's Business

Aboriginal girls and women have their own rituals and their own sacred sites, known as yawulyu (women's business). Among some tribes, women also have their own secret version of the Dreamtime myths unknown to the men and the children. In some areas, women also have their own separate camp, known as the jilimi. It is inhabited by widows, young single girls, and women who have temporarily left their husbands because of illness or disagreement. In addition to socializing and carrying out their daily tasks, the older women in the jilimi pass on religious knowledge and life skills to the younger ones.

This traditional Aboriginal painting *links pregnancy and childbirth to the Dreamtime, which is an explanation of the creation of the world and everything in it.*

Purified with Smoke

Aboriginal childbirth rituals are kept secret from children, younger women, and men, including the child's father, though a medicine man may be allowed to attend some stages of labor. Older women and those with children sing and dance around the birthing mother. The birth takes place away from the camp, with the woman's mother and another woman acting as midwives. Once the child is born, the baby and mother are secluded from the men for about five days. The child is then purified with smoke from a special fire.

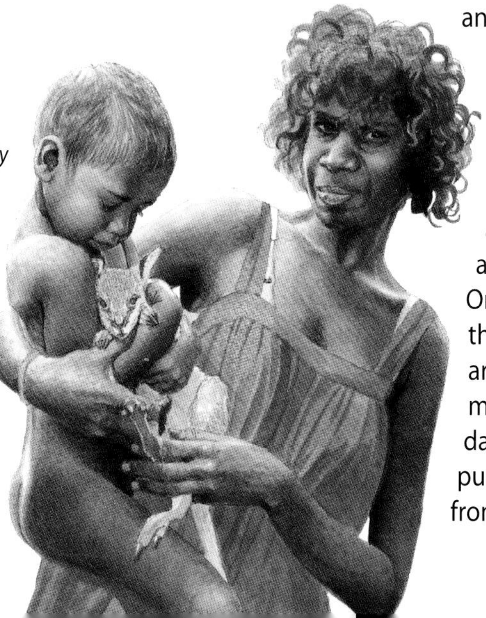

The Aboriginal population *declined rapidly from the late 1700's to the early 1900's, but it has now started to increase again.*

AUSTRALASIA AND OCEANIA

Australasia and Oceania lie east of Asia and west of the Americas. Australasia refers to Australia, New Guinea, New Zealand, and other nearby islands. New Guinea and New Zealand are also considered as part of the Pacific Islands, or Oceania. Oceania is a name given to a group of many thousands of islands scattered across the Pacific Ocean. New Guinea is the largest island in the group. It contains Irian Jaya, which is a part of Indonesia, and the independent country of Papua New Guinea. Islands near the mainland of Asia (Indonesia, Japan, the Philippines) are part of Asia. Islands near North and South America (the Aleutians, the Galapagos) are grouped with those continents. Australia is itself a continent.

DREAMTIME

The Australian Aborigines believe that the world and everything in it was created thousands of years ago in the Dreamtime, when their ancestors emerged from the earth and traveled across the land. These ancestors shaped the landscape. Then some went into the sky to become stars, while others stayed on the earth and became trees, rocks, animals, and birds. Although some knowledge of the Dreamtime is revealed to all Aborigines, complete knowledge is revealed only to boys as they grow into men.

These Aboriginal boys await their initiation ceremony with their male relatives. Their faces have been painted for the occasion.

Aboriginal Initiation Ceremonies for Boys

The details of initiation rituals for Aborigine boys vary from tribe to tribe. In general, however, boys are separated from their mothers at about age 10 and begin to live in the men's camp. Then, in a ceremony at puberty, they are circumcised, have a tooth knocked out, and sometimes have patterns cut on their chest, back, arms, and legs as a symbol of belonging both to their tribe and to the land they live on. They are then allowed to witness the secret rituals relating to the Dreamtime.

STORIES OF THE DREAMTIME were passed by word of mouth or in pictures painted on rocks or bark because Aborigines did not have a written language.

A male dancer from Papua New Guinea appears in ceremonial dress and face paint, below right.

Growing up in Papua New Guinea

In Papua New Guinea, on the island of New Guinea, girls become women without any ceremony, but boys must undergo an initiation ceremony before they are considered men. As there are many different tribes in the area, there are many different initiation ceremonies. Most involve some degree of pain, body scarring, and fear to prepare the initiates for the hardships of traditional life. In some tribes, adolescent boys are taken away from their female relations to sleep in the men's house, before going through a time of isolation in the spirit house, where they learn about their new lives as adults.

Maori Birth Rituals

When a Maori child is born, the father or a Maori priest recites a karakia (chanted prayer) so that supernatural power will be given to the child, who is accepted as a full member of the tribe from birth. Then a feast is held in celebration. This is especially important for the first-born child of a family. Sneezing at birth is thought to be a sign of a strong life force in a child.

New Zealand's Maoris take great pride in their culture and are trying to keep their traditions alive.

Glossary

Abandon To leave or give up a person or object.

Adulthood The time of life in which a person is fully grown.

Amulet An object, usually a piece of jewelry, inscribed with a magic spell or symbol and worn as a charm to ward off evil spirits or promote good luck.

Anoint To rub or apply a lotion, often oil, to the skin during a ceremony.

Blessing Divine favor or protection.

Caste One of the social classes into which Hindus are divided.

Congregation A gathering or assembly of people usually meeting to worship God or receive religious instruction.

Deity A god or goddess.

Destiny An imaginary power that determines the future events in someone's life.

Enlightenment The act of receiving spiritual or intellectual insight or information.

Fast To choose to go without eating for a time for religious reasons.

Fertility The ability to produce and reproduce things. Land is fertile when many crops can grow there.

Gratitude Thankfulness or the state of being pleased with something received.

Guardian A person who protects and takes care of another person or object.

Guru In Sikhism, one of 10 early leaders of religious faith. In Hinduism, a spiritual teacher.

Harmony An agreement of feelings, ideas, or actions, or an orderly arrangement.

Horoscope A diagram showing the position of the moon, sun, and planets at a specific time, such as when someone was born. A horoscope is used to predict events in someone's life.

Hygiene The maintenance of health and cleanliness in an individual person and within a group.

Icon An image of a god or deity that is considered sacred and is given special respect.

Incense A material made from gum or wood that produces perfumed smoke when it is burned.

Initiation The start or beginning of a process such as admission into a particular society or adult culture.

Insignia A distinguishing mark or symbol.

Intricate Complicated, with many twists and turns.

Jews Descendants of an ancient people called the Hebrews who practice Judaism.

Maturity The state at which a person becomes responsible for his or her actions and is able to make his or her own decisions.

Midwife A woman trained by schooling or experience who helps women in childbirth.

Migrate To move to a new area or country in search of work or better living conditions.

Minority A group of people with their own identity who are outnumbered by larger groups.

Monastery A place where a community of religious people, such as monks, live.

Monk A man who has separated himself from ordinary ways of life to devote himself to his religion.

Mortality The state of being subject to death. The mortality rate is the number of deaths that occur in a given time in a particular community.

Orphanage An institution that takes care of and provides shelter for children who have no parents and are homeless.

Pamper To treat and indulge someone with great care, attention, and love.

Penance A religious act that consists of the confession of sins and wrongdoings.

Persecute To pursue, punish, or harass a person or group of people. People might be persecuted because of religion, race, or gender.

Pilgrimage A journey taken to visit a holy place.

Puberty The stage during which a child physically develops into an adult.

Purification The act of cleansing a person or object, often through ceremony or ritual.

Recite To say something, like a prayer or verse, to an audience or in a group of people.

Regent A person who rules or governs a state or country in the absence or inability of the king or queen.

Rite of passage A ritual or ceremony associated with an event in a person's life that marks a change in status, such as becoming an adult.

Sacrament A Christian ceremony or practice that is symbolic of a person's faith and helps to bring God's blessing.

Sacred Holy or precious.

Sacrifice The killing of an animal, which is offered to a god or gods as part of worship.

Seclusion The condition of being removed and separated from the community and isolated from any social contact with others.

Shaman A priest or doctor who uses magic to protect people and to cure the sick.

Slaughter The killing of animals for food or ceremonial purposes.

Spirit A good or bad supernatural being or force.

Stalk To follow or hunt an animal without being seen for the purpose of observing, capturing, or killing it.

Symbolize To stand for or represent something else.

Ten Commandments Ten rules of life given to Moses by God on Mount Sinai and which all Jews and Christians are taught to follow.

Text A body of reading material.

Vision An unusual appearance of an image or a supernatural form.

Ward off To keep something away.

Wisdom The ability to judge what is right or true. Wisdom often develops with age and life experience.

Index